Super Simple Things to Do with Bubbles

Fun and Easy Science for Kids

Kelly Doudna

Consulting Editor, Diane Craig, M.A./Reading Specialist

A Division of ABDO

ABDO
Publishing Company

To Adult Helpers

Learning about science is fun and simple to do. There are just a few things to remember to keep kids safe. Some activities in this book recommend adult supervision. Some use sharp objects or hot objects. Be sure to review the activities before starting, and be ready to assist your budding scientist when necessary.

Key Symbols

In this book you will see some symbols. Here is what they mean.

 Hot. Get help! You will be working with something hot.

 Adult Help. Get help! You will need help from an adult.

 Sharp Object. Be careful! You will be working with a sharp object.

visit us at www.abdopublishing.com

Published by ABDO Publishing Company, a division of ABDO, P.O. Box 398166, Minneapolis, Minnesota 55439. Copyright © 2011 by Abdo Consulting Group, Inc. International copyrights reserved in all countries. No part of this book may be reproduced in any form without written permission from the publisher. Super SandCastle™ is a trademark and logo of ABDO Publishing Company.

Printed in the United States of America, North Mankato, Minnesota
102010
012011

 PRINTED ON RECYCLED PAPER

Editor: Liz Salzmann
Content Developer: Nancy Tuminelly
Cover and Interior Design and Production: Oona Gaarder-Juntti, Mighty Media, Inc.
Photo Credits: Kelly Doudna, Shutterstock
The following manufacturers/names appearing in this book are trademarks: Alka-Selzer®, Arm & Hammer®, Dawn®, Gedney®, McCormick®, Pyrex®, Schweppes®, Up & Up™

Library of Congress Cataloging-in-Publication Data

Doudna, Kelly, 1963-
  Super simple things to do with bubbles : fun and easy science for kids / Kelly Doudna.
    p. cm. -- (Super simple science)
  ISBN 978-1-61714-673-2
  1. Bubbles--Experiments--Juvenile literature. 2. Gases--Experiments--Juvenile literature. 3. Science--Experiments--Juvenile literature. I. Title.
  QC161.2.D68 2011
  541'.33078--dc22
                                2010020823

Super SandCastle™ books are created by a team of professional educators, reading specialists, and content developers around five essential components—phonemic awareness, phonics, vocabulary, text comprehension, and fluency—to assist young readers as they develop reading skills and strategies and increase their general knowledge. All books are written, reviewed, and leveled for guided reading, early reading intervention, and Accelerated Reader® programs for use in shared, guided, and independent reading and writing activities to support a balanced approach to literacy instruction.

Contents

Super Simple Science

Want to be a scientist? You can do it. It's super simple! Science is in things all around your house. Science is in a balloon and in a raisin. Science is in popcorn and in soda pop. Science is even in water and in dish soap. Science is everywhere. Try the **activities** in this book. You will find science right at home!

Bubbles

Learning about science using bubbles is super simple! Science explains why soap makes giant bubbles. Science explains why mixing two substances makes tiny gas bubbles. In this book, you will see how all kinds of bubbles can help you learn about science.

Work Like a Scientist

Scientists have a special way of working. It is a series of steps called the Scientific Method. Follow the steps to work like a scientist.

1. Look at something. Watch it. What do you see? What does it do?

2. Think of a question about the thing you are watching. What is it like? Why is it like that? How did it get that way?

3. Try to answer your question.

4. Do a test to find out if you are right. Write down what happened.

5. Think about it. Were you right? Why or why not?

Keep Track

Want to be just like a scientist? Scientists keep notes about everything they do. So, get a notebook. When you do an experiment, write down what happens in each step. It's super simple!

Materials

sugar

baking pan

white vinegar

measuring cup

balloons

food coloring

scissors

unpopped
popcorn kernels

utility knife

raisins

Alka-Seltzer tablet

bowls

eyedropper

yeast

6

clear plastic cups

hot glue gun

vegetable oil

hydrogen peroxide

straight
drinking straws

gallon
plastic jug

empty
plastic bottles

funnel

dish soap

measuring
spoons

dishwashing
detergent

baking soda

wax paper

club soda

Hip to Be Square

Is a square bubble cooler than a round one?

The soapy water sticks to the bubble frame. That makes a square bubble!

8

Part 1

1 Protect your work surface with a piece of wax paper. Use the hot glue gun to make a square out of four straw pieces. Make another square with four more straw pieces.

2 Use the remaining four straw pieces to join the two squares. Glue one end of each straw to a corner of one of the squares. The straw pieces should stick up.

3 Glue the corners of the other square to the other ends of the straws. Wait for the glue to dry. Then use scissors to cut off any extra glue. This is the bubble frame.

4 Have your adult helper cut off the top of the plastic jug.

5 Fill the plastic jug almost full with warm water. Add 1 cup (240 ml) of dish soap. Mix it gently with your hand.

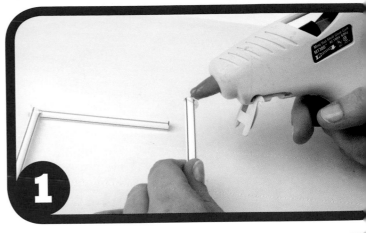

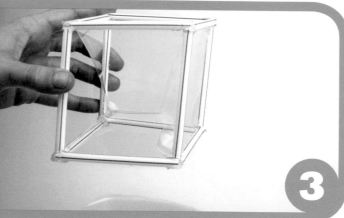

Part 2

1 Lower the bubble frame into the soap **mixture**. Push it down until it's completely covered.

2 Slowly pull the frame back out. How does it look?

3 Now, shake it gently. What happens?

4 Pull the rubber top off the eyedropper.

10

5 Dip the wide end of the dropper into the soap **mixture**. Gently blow through the small end to make a bubble.

6 Dunk the bubble frame again. Drop the round bubble into the top of the bubble frame. The round bubble should fall into the center of the square bubble. How does it look?

What's Going On?

Soap is **stretchy**. It sticks to the surface of water. When you blow into it, it stretches into a bubble. A natural bubble has a round shape. The soapy water also sticks to your bubble frame. That makes a square bubble. When you drop a round bubble onto the square bubble, it falls into the center. That makes a bubble within a bubble!

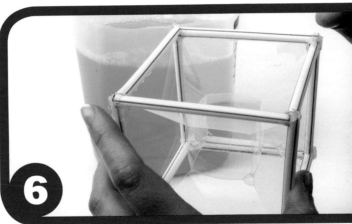

Popcorn Goes the Raisin

How strong are tiny bubbles?

Club soda bubbles lift the raisins and popcorn to the top.

1. Look closely at a raisin and a popcorn kernel. How are they different?

2. Drop three raisins into a cup of plain water. Drop three popcorn kernels into the other cup of plain water. Does anything happen? How about after a few minutes?

3. Drop three raisins into a cup of club soda. Drop three popcorn kernels into the other cup of club soda. What happens this time?

4. Keep watching the cups for a while. What do you observe?

What's Going On?

Bubbles form on the popcorn and raisins in both kinds of water. The bubbles in the plain water are very tiny. The bubbles in the club soda have carbon dioxide gas in them. They get larger. They make the popcorn kernels and raisins float. The bubbles pop. The raisins and kernels fall back to the bottom until new bubbles form.

The wrinkled raisins hold more bubbles than the smooth popcorn. So they rise to the surface faster.

13

Elephant's Toothpaste

Do you need to squeeze this bottle?

Yeast and hydrogen peroxide make a gas that creates bubbles.

What You'll Need
- measuring spoons
- measuring cups
- yeast
- water
- empty 16-ounce plastic bottle
- hydrogen peroxide
- dish soap (regular not antibacterial)
- food coloring
- funnel
- baking pan

Safety note

The bubbles look like toothpaste, but they are not safe to eat. Do not put them in your mouth! However, it is safe to touch the bubbles.

1. Put 1 teaspoon (5 ml) yeast and 2 tablespoons (30 ml) water in a small measuring cup. Stir until the yeast is **dissolved**.

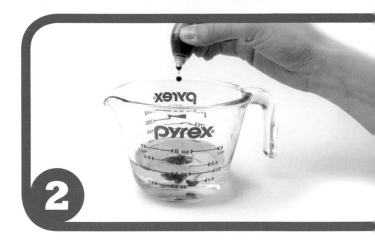

2. Have an adult helper measure ½ cup (118 ml) hydrogen peroxide. Add three or four drops of food coloring.

3. Stand the plastic bottle in the pan. Put the funnel in the top of the bottle. Pour the hydrogen peroxide **mixture** through the funnel.

4. Put a little dish soap in the bottle.

5. Pour the dissolved yeast into the bottle.

6. What happens? Touch the side of the bottle. How does it feel?

What's Going On?

Mixing yeast with the hydrogen peroxide causes a **chemical reaction**. The mixture makes a gas and bubbles up. It also gets warm. The bubbles look like toothpaste when they come out of the bottle.

15

That's Lava-ly!

Oil and water don't mix, but will they go with the flow?

The water and food coloring sink below the oil.

The Alka-Seltzer bubbles float up through the oil.

1. Fill the bottle three-quarters full with vegetable oil. Add water until the bottle is full.

2. Add ten drops of food coloring to the bottle.

3. Break the Alka-Seltzer tablet into eight pieces. Drop them into the bottle one at a time. Wait until the bubbling stops before you add the next one. What happens?

4. When the bubbling from the last piece stops, screw on the bottle cap. Tip the bottle back and forth. What does the **mixture** inside look like?

What's Going On?

Oil and water don't mix. The water sinks below the oil. So does the food coloring. When Alka-Seltzer **dissolves** in water, it makes tiny bubbles. The bubbles make the colored water float to the surface. At the surface, the bubbles pop. The colored water falls back to the bottom.

Soap du Jour

Can you turn soap into salt?

Carbon dioxide is released and salt remains.

1 Put 3 spoonfuls of powdered detergent in the bowl.

2 Add 1 spoonful of white vinegar.

3 **Swirl** the bowl to mix well. What happens?

What's Going On?

Mixing vinegar and soap causes a **chemical reaction**. That means the vinegar and soap combine and turn into other things. Bubbles of carbon dioxide are released from the **mixture**. A kind of salt is left behind.

Safety note

The salt left behind when the gas bubbles away is not safe to eat. Do not put it in your mouth!

It's a Gas, Gas, Gas!

How many ways can you blow up a balloon?

The yeast eats the sugar and releases gas bubbles. The bubbles fill the balloon.

The vinegar and baking soda cause a chemical reaction. Gas bubbles from the reaction fill the balloon.

Part 1

1 Blow up the balloons and let out the air. Do this to each balloon four or five times. This will **stretch** them out a little.

2 Put the yeast and 2 tablespoons (30 ml) of sugar in the measuring cup. Add enough hot water to make 1 cup (237 ml). Let the **mixture** sit for 2 minutes.

3 Pour the yeast mixture into one of the plastic bottles.

4 Quickly stretch one balloon over the top of the bottle. Check it every 30 minutes. What happens?

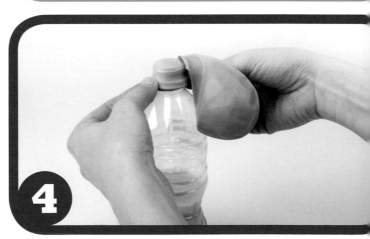

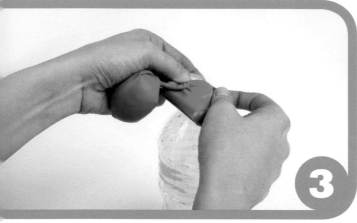

Part 2

1 Pour 1 tablespoon (15 ml) of vinegar into the second plastic bottle.

2 Put the funnel in the other balloon. Pour 1 teaspoon (5 ml) of baking soda through the funnel.

3 Twist the top of the balloon closed. Hold it closed while you **stretch** the mouth of the balloon over the mouth of the bottle.

4 Hold the balloon straight up. Untwist it so that the baking soda falls into the vinegar in the bottle. What happens? How does it compare with the yeast bottle?

22

What's Going On?

Yeast is a living **organism**. When you add warm water, the yeast feeds on the sugar. The yeast releases bubbles of gas as a result of eating. The gas slowly builds up inside the bottle. Then it starts filling the balloon.

Mixing baking soda and vinegar also produces gas bubbles. These bubbles are the result of a **chemical reaction**. They fill their bottle and blow up the balloon. They do it much faster than the yeast's gas bubbles.

 Conclusion

Congratulations! You found out that science can be super simple! And, you did it using different kinds of bubbles. Keep your thinking cap on. Where do you see bubbles every day?

 Glossary

activity – something you do for fun or to learn about something.

chemical reaction – when mixing two or more things together causes a change or makes a new substance.

congratulations – something you say to someone who has done well or accomplished something.

dissolve – to mix with a liquid so that it becomes part of the liquid.

mixture – a combination of two or more different things.

organism – a living thing, such as a plant, animal, or bacteria.

stretch – to get bigger or longer.

swirl – to whirl or to move smoothly in circles.